General Supplies

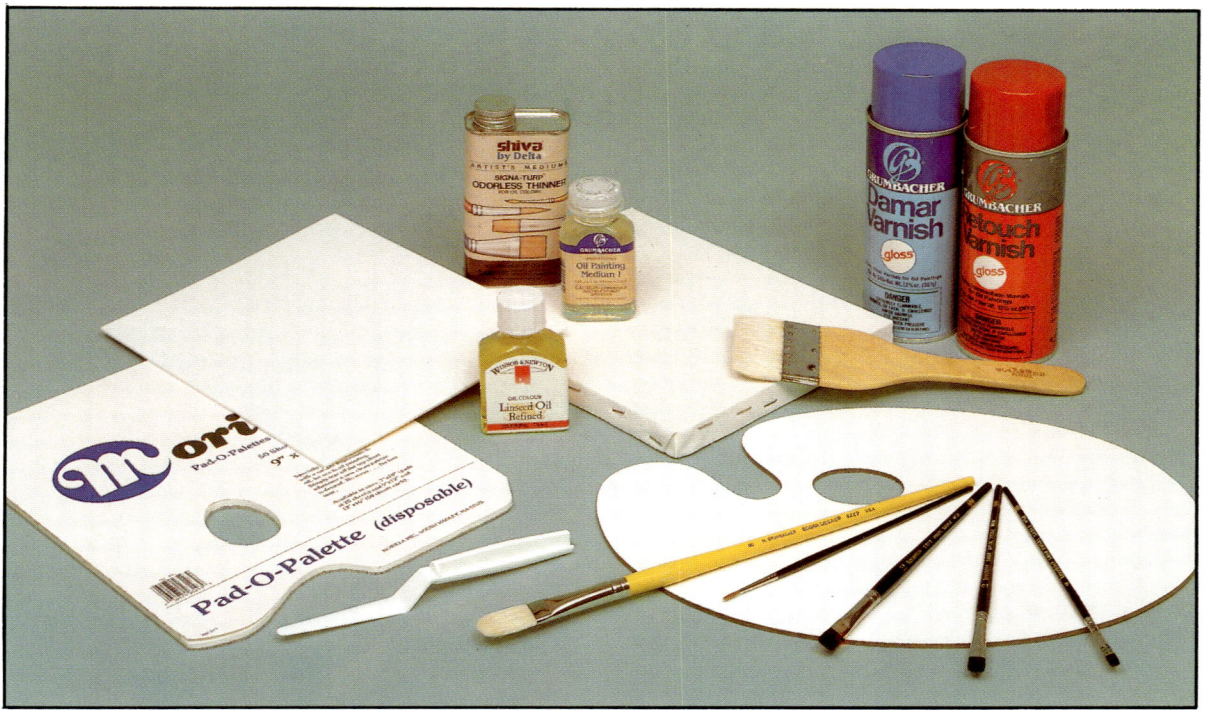

Brushes

There are so many different shapes and types of brushes available that it can sometimes be confusing. For example, a size #10 in one brand is not necessarily the same size as a #10 in another brand. The brushes I used on these projects are:

Grumbacher:
 #8 bristle filbert (Edgar Degas Series 4229)
 #1 sable or synthetic round

Langnickel Royal Sable Series 5010:
 #4 flat
 #10 flat
 #12 flat

Peacock or soft blender brush, 1" or 2½" (in the photo it is shown at upper right. It has a flat wooden handle and white bristles)

If Langnickel brushes are not available in your area, look for good synthetic flats. Your work is only as good as your brush. Don't skimp on your choice of brushes. It is an investment, but when well taken care of, the brushes will last a long time.

For general identification purposes, a flat brush has a square edge; a filbert brush has an oval shaped edge, and a round brush comes to a point. The drawing of the brush shows the various parts of the brush.

I generally like to use a bristle brush for my background and then use rounds and flats for the detail work.

Palette Knife

Most art supply stores now carry inexpensive palette knives that you can use for mixing your paint. They are made of plastic and are not as durable as the metal type. I prefer the ones with a bent handle because they are easier to mix with than the straight handle type.

Continued

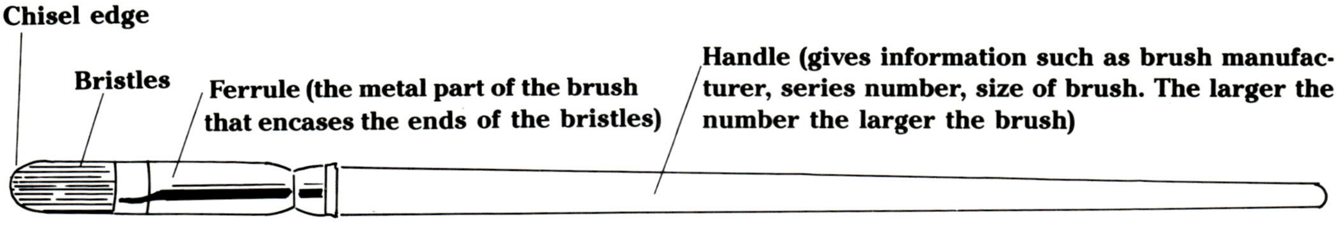

Chisel edge

Bristles

Ferrule (the metal part of the brush that encases the ends of the bristles)

Handle (gives information such as brush manufacturer, series number, size of brush. The larger the number the larger the brush)

General Supplies

Continued

Palette

I prefer to use disposable palette paper pads because of the convenience. They come in a variety of sizes. At the end of your painting project you can just tear off the page and throw it away. Some people use a piece of glass or wood on which to mix their paints. I find the clean-up of these messy and there is always the danger of the glass breaking.

Odorless Thinner

Use a good quality odorless thinner. It is best to purchase your thinner at an art supply store rather than a hardware store. Many times, the types found in hardware stores are not as refined as you need and it will be hard on your brush hairs. Odorless thinner is better for you than regular thinner from a health perspective, but still be sure you use it with adequate ventilation.

Oil Painting Medium

A painting medium is mixed with paint to make it a creamier consistency, make it transparent, or speed up the drying time. There are many different types but the one I generally use is refined linseed oil.

Intermediate and Final Varnish

Retouch Varnish by Grumbacher is used to give the painting a protective finish while drying. You may brush it on when the painting is dry or spray it on while the painting is still wet.

Damar Varnish, also by Grumbacher, was used as a final spray varnish when the painting is completely dry. It provides an even surface and protects the painting from dirt, moisture, and scuffing.

Other supplies

Paper towels
Tracing paper
Brush basin
Transfer paper or graphite paper
Black fine point permanent marker
Stylus
Masking tape

General Instructions

Before you get started please take some time to read over this entire section. It will make your oil painting experience much more enjoyable and successful.

Practice Makes Perfect

The basis of any successful painting is actually thinking and practicing. So practice as much as you can and don't put high expectations on yourself at the beginning. No one paints a masterpiece every time. The point is to have fun—painting definitely shouldn't be work! It will be rewarding to see your progress after only a few practice sessions. Unfortunately, it doesn't come overnight, but with determination and practice, you can paint beautiful pictures to be proud of.

Now for the thinking part. Sometimes I forget to think about what I'm painting and I just paint. That's when I invariably make mistakes. Most of the time I end up not getting my highlights or shadows in the right place. Always consider on which side of your painting the imaginary light source would be and place your highlights and shadows accordingly. Sometimes it's my stroke direction. For example, make sure your strokes for each petal are all going in the same direction. These are very important things to remember because with the proper highlighting and shading, along with the right color values, your painting will have depth and brilliance.

If you feel frustrated at any point, take a break, whether it's for fifteen minutes or an hour. Many times when you come back to your painting you will be able to see more clearly the area you are having trouble with. If that doesn't work, stand in front of a mirror holding your painting in front of you. Often this different perspective brings out the problem areas immediately.

I have found through my years of painting that most of the time if things don't look quite right it's because the highlights are not light enough or the shadows dark enough —or both! The great thing about painting with oils is that they have a long drying time, allowing you to rework the areas that need it. Remember that the painting is never done until you say it is done. Just keep working at it until you get it right.

Transferring the Patterns

Before beginning to paint, you need to transfer the pattern in this book to your canvas. First make a tracing of the pattern in the book onto tracing paper using a fine point black pen. Only trace the lines you feel you need. You can always refer back to the original pattern if necessary. In many of the patterns the leaves are covered up by the background color so it is best not to trace them.

Position the tracing on top of your canvas and center it. Secure it with masking tape at the top and one side. Lift

General Instructions

the tracing paper up where it is not taped and slide a piece of graphite or tracing paper underneath with the inked side down. Re-trace the lines lightly with a stylus. Note: Do not use carbon paper to transfer with. The lines are too dark and are very hard to cover or remove. Now you are ready to paint!

Placing Colors on Your Palette

When placing colors on your palette, squirt out a small amount at a time. Oil paints are very pigmented so a little color goes a long way. Try to group similar colors together, such as all yellows, reds, or blues for example.

Squirt the colors out along the edge of the palette. This allows the middle area of the palette to be used for mixing. After squirting out the colors, you can label them by writing their names with a black marker next to the color. This will help you to start associating the color name with the color.

Mixing Colors

If the color you are mixing is light, begin first with the lightest colors in the mixture and then add the darker color(s) to it a little at a time, mixing well with the palette knife. If you add too much of the dark color, don't keep adding more light color. If you do you will end up with a big pile of paint that you won't use and there's no reason to waste paint. It's best to start over mixing a new puddle.

If the color you are mixing is dark, start first with the darkest colors in the mixture and add the lighter colors to it.

When you are mixing colors, be sure to wipe off your palette knife well on a paper towel before dipping into another color.

If your color puddle seems too thick, simply add a few drops of linseed oil and work it into the color with the palette knife.

Holding the Brush

Hold your brush lightly in your hand as far back on the handle as possible. If you grip the brush too low (like holding a pencil) you will have too much pressure when applying the paint.

Loading the Brush

A properly loaded brush is very important. To load your brush, dip it into the paint on the palette at a 45 degree angle on the outer edge of the color puddle. Drag the brush away from the color, flip the brush over, and repeat on the other side.

Find a clean space on your palette and stroke the brush up and down in a 2" section. This helps work the paint into the bristles evenly. An evenly loaded brush will hold the chisel edge well which is important for smooth edges on your flowers.

Avoid dipping your brush into the center of the color puddle. This could cause paint to get up on the ferrule of the brush. If this happens repeatedly the paint will get trapped under the ferrule and will cause damage to the bristles.

Cleaning Your Brushes

Proper care of your brushes is very important to their long life. The first step is to wipe out excess paint on a paper towel. When doing this, do not tug on the bristles.

Next, clean the brush as much as possible with odorless thinner. Then wash the brush with mild soap and warm water. NEVER use hot water. With the soap in the palm of your hand, use either an "X" stroke or a circular motion with the brush directly on the soap until all leftover color comes out of the brush. Wipe the brush dry and shape the hairs back to their original shape.

Always lay brushes on their sides to dry. If you stand them upright, any leftover residue could become trapped in the ferrule, causing the bristles to lose their shape. If you need to store your brushes upright, make sure they are dry before doing so.

Periodically you will need to condition your brushes. After cleaning, put some lard oil on your brush and reshape the bristles, allowing the oil to stay in the brush while it is drying. Just remember to clean the brush in odorless thinner before painting again to remove the oil.

There are also many good brush cleaners and conditioners on the market that you can use, such as Brush Plus™ from Plaid Enterprises.

Finishing

When your painting is finished, it's a good idea to give it a coat of Retouch Varnish to provide a protective coating while it is thoroughly drying. You can brush on the varnish when the painting is dry to the touch or spray on a light coat when it is still wet.

Oil paintings may take up to a year or more to dry thoroughly depending on how much paint is used and the climate. After a year, or when the painting is completely dry, spray or brush on a coat of final Damar Varnish. It comes in a gloss or matte finish so you can choose which is the most appropriate and appealing to you.

Whenever you spray your painting (intermediate or final varnish), be sure to work in an adequately ventilated area. I generally wait for a calm, sunny day and set my painting and can of varnish outside so they warm up to the same temperature. This allows for better adhesion. Always remember to spray lightly and follow the instructions on the cans.

Helpful Hints and Tips

- Blending colors: When colors need to be blended together to create another color, this is indicated by a plus (+) sign.
- If you feel that you are getting too much paint on the canvas, you can either let it dry or take a palette knife or a paper towel and lift up the paint in that particular **Continued**

General Instructions

Continued

area. You may need to apply a bit more of your basecoat color before working up your highlights and shadows.

- Do not leave your brush with the bristles down in a container for any length of time. The bristles will take on the shape of the bottom of the container. Products such as the Brush Basin® from Plaid Enterprises suspend brushes in solutions without bending or distorting the bristles and are very handy items.

- Be very careful to not use too much oil painting medium in your paints or you will find that the paints slide on top of each other instead of sticking. I generally mix a couple of drops of medium into my paint with the palette knife if the paint seems too thick.

- If you wish to speed up the drying time of your painting, add sun-thickened linseed oil to your paint. You may also need to add a few drops of clean odorless thinner to maintain the proper paint consistency.

- When choosing paper towels, the most expensive ones may not always be the best. I have had students buy expensive paper towels and end up with a lot of lint in their wet paint. Just choose a paper towel that is lint free. Also, watch out for paper towels with a lot of texture. These can be very hard on the bristles of your sable brushes when wiping them off.

General Painting Instructions

Painting Techniques and Terms

Wet-On-Wet
The paintings in this book are all painted with the wet-on-wet technique. This means that once the painting is started, you will work at it until it is done. In this way, all the colors can be blended together smoothly, giving the painting a soft look.

If you have to let a painting dry and then come back to it, it may be hard to achieve a soft look since you will be painting wet color over dry color and it is very hard to blend.

Basecoat
This is simply covering any indicated area with a solid coverage of color. Remember to use as little paint as possible when basecoating because you will be layering a lot of colors on top. The less paint underneath, the easier it will be to blend the colors that go over.

Highlight
Highlights are painted with light colors to bring out areas where light would naturally fall.

Shading
Shaded areas are painted with darker colors for added depth and dimension as well as to create shadow areas.

Blended Flower Petals

The petals for the violets, poppies, pansies, hibiscus, and the bottom section of the peonies and iris are all painted in the following manner. Refer to the color worksheets for further detail.

1. Fill in the basecoat color of the flowers using the brush and color indicated in the project instructions.
2. Pull the shadows from the inside of the petal toward the outside or highlighted edge.
3. Pull the highlights from the outside edge toward the center. Move over approximately half a brush width as you paint, following the arrows on pattern or color worksheets where appropriate for the proper stroke direction.
4. Do not pull your highlights in so far toward the center that you lose your basecoat color. Use a light pressure and stay up on the chisel edge of your brush, painting with a light sweeping motion.

Painting Leaves

The leaves for the pansies, roses, poppies, hibiscus, mums, peonies, daisies, and violets are all painted in the following manner. Refer to the color worksheets for further detail.

1. Using the basecoat color and brush specified in the project instructions, begin painting the leaf at the base (the broadest part). Begin the stroke at the outside edge and angle in toward the center of the leaf at a 45 degree angle.
2. As you near the top of the leaf, you will continue to paint at a 45 degree angle but use a shorter stroke. Repeat for the other side of the leaf in the same manner.
3. When stroking, move the brush over only half a brush width as you go.
4. If shading is called for, use the same technique with the color indicated.
5. If a highlight is called for, do not pull the stroke in all the way to the center. Only pull the brush about halfway to the center, allowing some of the basecoat color to show through. When finished, the strokes on the leaves will resemble the letter "V". Use very little pressure on the brush on the chisel edge.
6. Apply the vein with the highlight colors, using the chisel edge of the brush at a 90 degree angle to the canvas.

Note: The geranium leaves have strokes that radiate from the outside edge toward the center point. Iris leaves are, for the most part, blended up and down.

Techniques Color Worksheet

Basecoating—Right Way
Base in color solidly unless instructions direct you to mix thinner with it. Color should be applied evenly and should not be thick.

Basecoating—Wrong Way
Basecoat color was applied too lightly. It appears blotchy.

Highlighting—Right Way
Highlight petals with color, moving over half a brush width each time. This allows the colors to blend together.

Highlighting—Wrong Way
Brush was moved over a full brush width, causing petal to look streaked.

Highlight Direction—Right Way
Highlight petals from the outside edge and pull stroke towards the center of each petal. Allow some of the base color to show through towards the center of each petal.

Highlight Direction—Wrong Way
Color was pulled too far into the center of the petal, covering up the base color.

Blending—Right Way
Place two colors side-by-side and stroke colors where they meet. Gradually stroke towards the lighter color until you have a smooth transition.

Blending—Wrong Way
Color was not blended properly. This example needs more blending for a smoother color transition

7

Iris Color Worksheet

1. **Basecoat with Floral Mauve, Permanent Blue, and Winsor Violet.** Add a bit of oil medium to these colors as you go. Add the lightest color at the tip of petals and curved areas, and the darkest color in the shadowed areas and base of petals. Do not mix these colors together on palette. Blend each into the other on the canvas.

2. **Highlight with Permanent Rose + White.** Add additional highlights of White. Pull the strokes in the direction of the arrows. Tap on the beards with Floral Mauve and Winsor Violet.

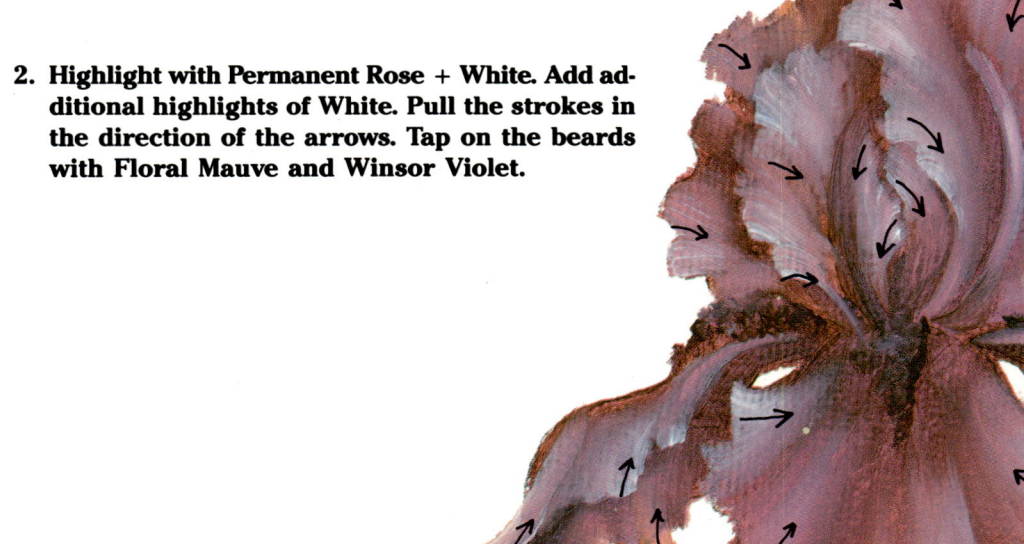

Iris–Eye of Heaven

Pattern on Pattern Sheet
Pictured on Page 8

Materials
16" x 20" canvas
Palette:
  FolkArt Acrylic—
    Parrot Green
  Permalba—
    Floral Mauve
  Winsor Newton—
    Winsor Violet
    Permanent Rose
    Olive Green
  Grumbacher—
    Soft Formula Titanium White
    Chromium Oxide Green
    Cerulean Blue
    Cadmium Yellow Light
Brushes:
  #10 flat

Instructions
(See Iris Color Worksheet for painting detail.)
1. Transfer pattern to canvas.
2. Basecoat outside of the oval with Parrot Green using a large brush.
3. Basecoat the green leaves with Chromium Oxide Green and shade with a mixture of Olive Green + Winsor Violet. Highlight with Cadmium Yellow Light + Chromium Oxide Green, then Cadmium Yellow Light + White, and finally with Cerulean Blue + White.
4. Basecoat the blue leaves and stem with a mixture of Cerulean Blue + a bit of White + a bit of Chromium Oxide Green. Highlight by adding more White to the above mix and shade with Floral Mauve and Winsor Violet where indicated on pattern.
5. Fill in the iris and bud first with Floral Mauve, then Permanent Rose, and then Winsor Violet. Add a bit of oil medium to each of the colors above. Be careful to stroke the petals following the direction of the arrows on the pattern.
6. Highlight the flowers with Permanent Rose + White, then with White.
7. Tap in the beards using the corner of the #10 flat brush and first Floral Mauve and then Winsor Violet.
8. Let dry and varnish according to General Instructions.

The Rose – Queen of Flowers

Instructions on Page 13

Rose Color Worksheet

1. Basecoat with Light Magenta mixed with a bit of odorless thinner.

2. Shade base of petals with a mixture of Burnt Alizarin + Floral Mauve + a bit of Permanent Blue.

3. Highlight petal tips with Brilliant Yellow Light.

4. Basecoat leaves with Sap Green + a bit of Burnt Sienna. Highlight with a mixture of Sap Green + Indian Yellow + a bit of White. Pull the strokes in the direction of the arrows.

5. Add additional highlights of Indian Yellow + White and Cadmium Orange + White.

The Rose— Queen of Flowers

**Pattern on Pattern Sheet
Pictured on Page 11**

Materials
9" x 12" canvas
Palette:
  Shiva—
    Brilliant Yellow Light
    Ice Blue
    Flesh
  Grumbacher—
    Soft Formula Titanium White
    Sap Green
    Alizarin Crimson
    Cadmium Yellow Light
Brushes:
  Blender
  #8 bristle filbert
  #4 flat
  #10 flat

Instructions

(See Rose Color Worksheet for flower and leaf details.)

1. Transfer pattern to canvas.
2. Using a #8 bristle filbert brush, fill in the background with Ice Blue. Be sure to fill in all leaf areas also.
3. Add "X" strokes of Flesh to the right of the roses and then add Sap Green + a touch of Alizarin Crimson around the design area. Blend out over the background until the colors fade together. Soften with a blender brush.
4. Basecoat the larger leaves according to General Instructions using Sap Green + a touch of Alizarin Crimson and a #10 flat brush.
5. Highlight the leaves with White + Cadmium Yellow Light + Sap Green + a touch of Alizarin Crimson, then White + Cadmium Yellow Light, and finally with White + Alizarin Crimson + a touch of Sap Green. Leave the leaves darker in the shadow areas as indicated by cross hatches on the pattern.
6. Paint the small leaves using a #4 flat brush and a mixture of Sap Green + a touch of Alizarin Crimson.
7. Paint the stems and calyx the same colors as the large leaves.
8. Basecoat the bottom rose with Alizarin Crimson + a touch of Sap Green + a bit of odorless thinner. Highlight with Brilliant Yellow Light.
9. Basecoat the top and center rose with White + Alizarin Crimson + a touch of Sap Green + a bit of odorless thinner. Shade with Alizarin Crimson + Sap Green where indicated on pattern. Highlight with Brilliant Yellow Light.
10. Let dry and varnish according to General Instructions.

Roses and Lilacs

Pattern on Pattern Sheet

Materials
12" x 16" canvas
Palette:
  Permalba—
    Misty Grey
    Floral Mauve
    Burnt Alizarin
  Shiva—
    Brilliant Yellow Light
  Liquitex—
    Light Magenta
  Grumbacher—
    Sap Green
    Cerulean Blue
    Permanent Blue
    Cadmium Yellow Light
Brushes:
  Blender
  #8 bristle filbert
  #4 flat
  #10 flat
  #1 round

Instructions

(See Rose Color Worksheet for flower and leaf detail.)

1. Transfer pattern to canvas.
2. Using a #8 bristle filbert brush apply Misty Grey to the background, going over the areas where the lilacs and leaves will be painted. In the corners add a mixture of Burnt Alizarin + Floral Mauve + a bit of Permanent Blue. Use "X" strokes and very little paint on your brush.
3. Add a mixture of Sap Green + a bit of Burnt Alizarin around the design area, again using very little paint on the brush. Blend out from this area into the Misty Grey until the color fades into the Misty Grey. Soften with a blender brush.
4. Fill in the lilac area with "X" strokes using a #4 flat brush and a mixture of Floral Mauve + Burnt Alizarin + a bit of Permanent Blue.
5. Add small four-stroke flowers on top of the lilac area with a mixture of Light Magenta + Brilliant Yellow Light. Randomly add centers to the small flowers with a small dot of Cadmium Yellow Light using a #1 round brush.
6. Basecoat the larger leaves according to General Instructions using a #10 flat brush and a mixture of Sap Green + a bit of Burnt Alizarin.
7. Highlight the leaves with Brilliant Yellow Light + Cadmium Yellow Light + the leaf basecoat mix and then with Brilliant Yellow Light + Cerulean Blue. Leave the base of the leaves darker as indicated by cross hatches on the pattern.
8. Paint the small leaves with a #4 flat brush using the leafbasecoat mixture.
9. Add the stems and calyx with the same colors as the large leaves using the chisel edge of a #10 flat brush.
10. Basecoat the roses using a #10 flat brush and Light Magenta with a bit of odorless thinner added to it.
11. Shade the roses where indicated on the pattern by cross hatches with a mixture of Burnt Alizarin + Floral Mauve + a bit of Permanent Blue.
12. Highlight the roses with Brilliant Yellow Light.
13. Let dry and varnish according to General Instructions.

The Magic of the Poppy

The Magic of the Poppy

Pattern on Pattern Sheet

Materials
9" x 12" canvas
Palette:
  Shiva—
    Brilliant Yellow Light
  Permalba—
    Misty Grey
  Grumbacher—
    Soft Formula Titanium White
    Cadmium Yellow Medium
    Cadmium Red Light
    Grumbacher Red
    Sap Green
    Cerulean Blue
    Alizarin Crimson
Brushes:
  Blender
  #8 bristle filbert
  #12 flat
  #4 flat

Instructions

1. Transfer pattern to canvas.
2. Using a #8 bristle filbert brush, fill in the background with Misty Grey. Apply the color over the area where the leaves go as they will be painted on top of the basecoat.
3. Now using a #12 flat brush and a mixture of Sap Green + a touch of Alizarin Crimson (use very little paint), go all around the flowers on top of the Misty Grey. Use "X" strokes, working the color out so it fades into the Misty Grey. Soften with a blender brush.
4. Paint the larger leaves according to the General Instructions using a #12 flat brush and a mixture of Sap Green + a touch of Alizarin Crimson.
5. Highlight the leaves with a mixture of Sap Green + Cadmium Yellow Medium + White and then White + Cerulean Blue. Add touches of Alizarin Crimson here and there using very little paint on the brush.
6. Paint the small leaves with a #4 flat brush and a mixture of Sap Green + a touch of Alizarin Crimson.
7. Paint the stems and calyx the same colors as the larger leaves.
8. Basecoat the poppies using a #12 flat brush and Grumbacher Red + a bit of odorless thinner.
9. Shade the flowers where indicated on the pattern by cross hatches with a mixture of Alizarin Crimson + a touch of Sap Green.
10. Highlight the poppies with White + Cadmium Yellow Medium + a touch of Cadmium Red Light, then White + a touch of Cerulean Blue, and finally with Brilliant Yellow Light.
11. Tap in the flower centers using the corner of a #12 flat brush with Alizarin Crimson + a touch of Sap Green.
12. Let dry and varnish according to General Instructions.

The Yellow Hibiscus

Pattern on Pattern Sheet

Materials
9" x 12" canvas
Palette:
  Winsor Newton—
    Winsor Violet
    Indian Yellow
  Shiva—
    Flesh
    Brilliant Yellow Light
  Grumbacher—
    Burnt Sienna
    Alizarin Crimson
    Burnt Umber
    Yellow Ochre
    Cadmium Orange
    Sap Green
Brushes:
  Blender
  #8 bristle filbert
  #10 flat
  #4 flat
  #1 round

Instructions

(See Hibiscus Color Worksheet for flower detail.)

1. Transfer pattern to canvas.
2. Using a #8 bristle filbert, apply the background with Burnt Sienna + a touch of Alizarin Crimson + a bit of oil medium. Darken the corners and under the flowers with Burnt Umber.
3. Highlight background above and below the peach flower (on the right) with a mixture of Brilliant Yellow Light + Cadmium Orange + Yellow Ochre. Soften with a blender brush.
4. Basecoat the leaves according to the General Instructions using a mixture of Sap Green + a bit of Burnt Sienna.
5. Using a #10 flat brush, highlight the leaves with Sap Green + Indian Yellow + Brilliant Yellow Light, then Brilliant Yellow Light + Indian Yellow, and finally with Sap Green + Indian Yellow + Cadmium Orange. Note the darker areas on the leaves indicated by cross hatches on the pattern. Refer to photograph.
6. Stroke in the violets using a #4 flat brush and a mixture of Winsor Violet + a bit of Burnt Sienna.
7. Highlight the violets with Brilliant Yellow Light + Winsor Violet + a touch of Burnt Sienna.
8. Tap in a dot of Brilliant Yellow Light + Indian Yellow in the center of the open violets. Place a comma stroke on each side of the dot with Brilliant Yellow Light using a #1 round brush.
9. Basecoat the peach hibiscus (on the right) using a #10 flat brush and a mixture of Brilliant Yellow Light + Yellow Ochre + Cadmium Orange.
10. Shade the peach hibiscus where indicated on the pattern by cross hatches with Cadmium Orange + a touch of Burnt Sienna. Highlight with Flesh and Brilliant Yellow Light. Follow the direction of the arrows on the pattern for highlights.
11. Basecoat the yellow hibiscus (on the left) using a #10 flat brush and Indian Yellow + a bit of odorless thinner.
12. Shade the yellow hibiscus where indicated on the pattern with Yellow Ochre + a touch of Burnt Sienna. Highlight with Brilliant Yellow Light, again following the direction of the arrows on the pattern.
13. Paint in the stamens using the chisel edge of a #4 flat brush and Cadmium Orange + a touch of Burnt Sienna. Highlight with Brilliant Yellow Light + a touch of Indian Yellow.
14. Tap on the ends of the stamens with the corner of a #4 flat brush and Cadmium Orange + Burnt Sienna, then Brilliant Yellow Light + Indian Yellow, and finally Brilliant Yellow Light.
15. Let dry and varnish according to General Instructions.

Scarlet Hibiscus

Pattern on Pattern Sheet

Materials
12" x 16" canvas
Palette:
  Permalba—
    Misty Grey
  Liquitex—
    Light Magenta
  Shiva—
    Ice Blue
  Grumbacher—
    Soft Formula Titanium White
    Cadmium Red Light
    Alizarin Crimson
    Sap Green
    Cerulean Blue
    Cadmium Yellow Light
Brushes:
  Blender brush
  #8 bristle filbert
  #12 flat

Instructions

(See Hibiscus Color Worksheet for details on flower.)

1. Transfer pattern to canvas.
2. Paint the background area, even over the leaf areas, using a #8 bristle filbert and Misty Grey. Soften with a blender brush.
3. Basecoat the leaves according to General Instructions using a #12 flat brush and Sap Green + a bit of Alizarin Crimson.
4. Highlight the leaves with White + Cadmium Yellow Light + Sap Green, then with Cerulean Blue + White, and finally with Light Magenta + White.
5. Basecoat the pink bud at the top with Light Magenta using a #12 flat brush. Shade with Alizarin Crimson + a touch of Sap Green where indicated by cross hatches on the pattern. Highlight with White and lightly tint with Cadmium Red Light.
6. Basecoat the white bud at the bottom right with Ice Blue using a #12 flat brush. Shade with Alizarin Crimson + a touch of Sap Green where indicated and highlight with White.
7. Basecoat the red hibiscus using Cadmium Red Light with a bit of odorless thinner added using a #12 flat brush. Shade with a mixture of Alizarin Crimson + a touch of Sap Green where indicated on the pattern and highlight with Light Magenta + White and then more White.
8. Paint in the stamen with the chisel edge of a #12 flat brush using Cadmium Red Light + Cadmium Yellow Light + White. Place a shadow underneath the stamen with Alizarin Crimson + a touch of Sap Green.
9. Highlight the stamen with Cadmium Yellow Light + White. Tap on the dots at the end of the stamen with the corner of a #12 flat brush using all of the paint mixtures used on the stamen.
10. Let dry and varnish according to General Instructions.

Hibiscus Color Worksheet

1. Basecoat with Cadmium Red Light + a bit of odorless thinner.

2. Shade with a mixture of Alizarin Crimson plus a touch of Sap Green. Pull the strokes in the direction of the arrows.

3. Highlight with a mixture of Light Magenta + White. Add additional highlights of White. Pull the strokes in the direction of the arrows.

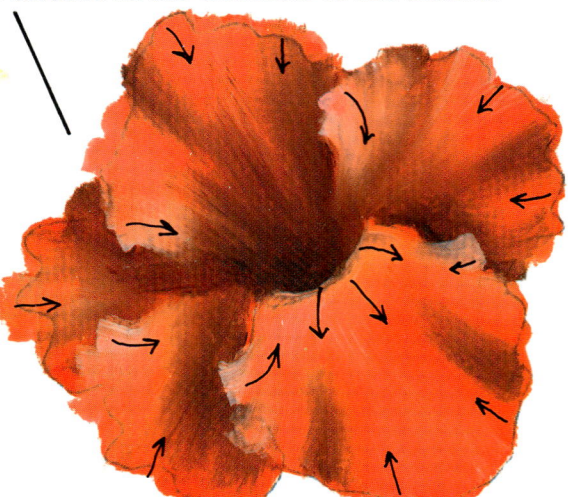

4. Paint in the stamen with a mixture of Cadmium Red Light + Cadmium Yellow Light + a touch of White. Place a shadow underneath the stamen with Alizarin Crimson + a touch of Sap Green. Highlight with Cadmium Yellow Light + White. Tap on the dots at the end of the stamen with all previously listed colors in this step.

Pansy Color Worksheet

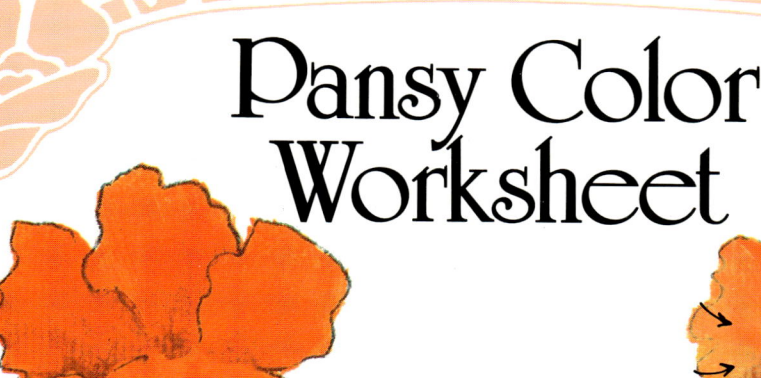

1. Basecoat with Cadmium Orange + a bit of Burnt Sienna. Shade by adding more Burnt Sienna to the basecoat mixture.

2. Add highlights of Cadmium Orange + Indian Yellow + White. Add additional highlights with Indian Yellow + White. Pull the strokes in the direction of the arrows.

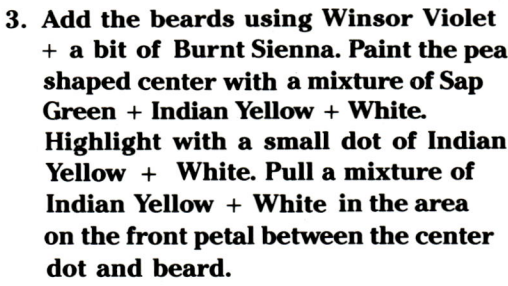

3. Add the beards using Winsor Violet + a bit of Burnt Sienna. Paint the pea shaped center with a mixture of Sap Green + Indian Yellow + White. Highlight with a small dot of Indian Yellow + White. Pull a mixture of Indian Yellow + White in the area on the front petal between the center dot and beard.

5. Highlight leaf with a mixture of Sap Green + Indian Yellow + a touch of White. Add additional highlights with Indian Yellow + White and Cadmium Orange + White. Pull the vein through the leaf using the highlight colors. Shade under the vein with Sap Green + a touch of Burnt Sienna. Pull the strokes in the direction of the arrows.

4. Basecoat leaf with a mixture of Sap Green + a touch of Burnt Sienna.

23

The Pansy of Love

The Pansy of Love

Pattern on Pattern Sheet

Materials

11" x 14" canvas
Palette:
  Winsor Newton—
    Winsor Violet
    Indian Yellow
  Shiva—
    Brilliant Yellow Light
  Grumbacher—
    Cadmium Orange
    Burnt Sienna
    Sap Green
    Burnt Umber

Brushes:
  Blender
  #8 bristle filbert
  #4 flat
  #10 flat
  #1 round

Instructions

(See Pansy Color Worksheet for flower and leaf detail.)

1. Transfer pattern to canvas.
2. Paint the background with Burnt Sienna with a bit of oil medium added to it using a #8 bristle filbert brush.
3. Darken the corners and underneath the basket with Burnt Umber. Soften with a blender brush.
4. Basecoat the basket with Indian Yellow + a bit of Burnt Sienna + a bit of oil medium. Darken the edges and bottom of the basket with Indian Yellow + a bit of Burnt Sienna.
5. Using a #10 flat brush on the chisel edge turned to the side, add the woven lines of the basket with Brilliant Yellow Light. Remember to keep the curve to the basket and not to pull the lines straight across. Make both vertical and horizontal lines with bolder strokes at the bottom of the basket. See photograph.
6. Tap in the soft foliage areas using the corner of a #10 flat brush and a mixture of Sap Green + Burnt Sienna. Tap clusters of flowers over the foliage using Brilliant Yellow Light + Indian Yellow, and then Winsor Violet + a bit of Burnt Sienna + Brilliant Yellow Light.
7. Basecoat the leaves according to the General Instructions using a mixture of Sap Green + a bit of Burnt Sienna.
8. Highlight the leaves using a #10 flat brush and Brilliant Yellow Light + Indian Yellow, then Brilliant Yellow Light + Indian Yellow + a bit of Sap Green, and finally Brilliant Yellow Light + Cadmium Orange. Leave the areas indicated on the pattern by cross hatches darker.
9. Paint the calyx on the flowers the same colors as the leaves.
10. Basecoat the orange buds and center pansy using a #4 flat brush and Cadmium Orange + a bit of Burnt Sienna. Stroke from the outside edge toward the center following the direction of the arrows on the pattern.
11. Shade these flowers using a bit more Burnt Sienna in the basecoat mixture where indicated on the pattern by cross hatches.
12. Highlight the flowers with Brilliant Yellow Light + Indian Yellow. The front three petals of the center pansy have a mixture of Winsor Violet + a touch of Burnt Sienna stroked from the center out onto the petal at uneven lengths using a #1 round brush.
13. Place a small dot of Brilliant Yellow Light + Indian Yellow + Sap Green in the pansy centers. Highlight the center with a smaller dot of Brilliant Yellow Light + Indian Yellow.
14. Basecoat the yellow buds and the remaining two pansies with Indian Yellow that has a bit of odorless thinner added to it using a #4 flat brush.
15. Shade these flowers with a mixture of Indian Yellow + a bit of Burnt Sienna. Highlight with Brilliant Yellow Light.
16. Finish off the centers of the pansies the same as for the center pansy.
17. Let dry and varnish according to General Instructions.

Summer Geraniums

Summer Geraniums

Pattern on Pattern Sheet

Materials
12" x 24" canvas
Palette:
  Winsor Newton—
    Olive Green
  Permalba—
    Misty Grey
    Burnt Alizarin
    Floral Pink
  Grumbacher—
    Soft Formula Titanium White
    Alizarin Crimson
    Grumbacher Red
    Cadmium Red Light
    Cadmium Yellow Pale
    Cadmium Orange
    Chromium Oxide Green
    Cerulean Blue
Brushes:
  Blender
  #8 bristle filbert
  #10 flat
  #12 flat
  #1 round

Instructions
1. Transfer pattern to canvas.
2. Paint the background around the design using a #8 bristle filbert and Misty Grey using "X" strokes. Pick up some Burnt Alizarin and add "X" strokes on the corners and randomly over the background area. Soften with a blender brush.
3. Basecoat the leaves using a #12 flat brush and just enough Chromium Oxide Green to cover the canvas. You do not want to use a lot of paint because you will by layering shadows and highlights over the leaves.
4. Shade the leaves with Olive Green, using the chisel edge of a #12 flat brush. Highlight with Cadmium Orange, then Cerulean Blue, and finally with Cadmium Yellow Pale + White.
5. Paint the stems the same colors as the leaves. Stroke the color across the stems instead of up and down.
6. Basecoat the geraniums with Burnt Alizarin + a bit of Alizarin Crimson.
7. Add petal strokes using a #10 flat brush and Grumbacher Red. Highlight the flowers with Cerulean Blue, then Cadmium Red Light, then Cadmium Yellow Pale + White, and finally with Cadmium Orange + White.
8. Add dots in the centers of the flowers using a #1 round brush and Cadmium Yellow Pale. Add a line under these centers with Burnt Alizarin.
9. Let dry and varnish according to General Instructions.

Peony – The Rose of Spring

Peony–
The Rose of Spring

Pattern on Pattern Sheet

Materials
11" x 14" canvas
Palette:
  Permalba—
    Misty Grey
    Burnt Alizarin
    Floral Mauve
  Liquitex—
    Light Magenta
  Shiva—
    Brilliant Yellow Light
  Grumbacher—
    Sap Green
    Cadmium Yellow Light
    Cerulean Blue
    Cadmium Orange
    Permanent Blue
Brushes:
  Blender
  #8 bristle filbert
  #4 flat
  #10 flat
  #12 flat
  #1 round

Instructions

1. Transfer pattern to canvas.
2. Paint the background using a #8 bristle filbert brush and Misty Grey, going over the leaf and small mauve flower areas.
3. Make "X" strokes around the design edge with a mixture of Sap Green + a bit of Burnt Alizarin. Use very little paint on your brush. Blend the color out over the gray so it fades away. Soften with a blender brush.
4. Basecoat the larger leaves according to General Instructions using a #12 flat brush and a mixture of Sap Green + a touch of Burnt Alizarin.
5. Highlight the leaves with Brilliant Yellow Light + a touch of Cerulean Blue, then with Brilliant Yellow Light + a touch of Cadmium Yellow Light, and finally with Brillant Yellow Light + a touch of Cadmium Orange.
6. Paint the calyx and stems the same colors as the leaves. Paint the stems using the chisel edge of a #10 flat brush.
7. Paint the small leaves with a #4 flat brush and the leaf basecoat mixture.
8. Basecoat the small flowers with Burnt Alizarin on some and a mixture of Burnt Alizarin + a bit of Floral Mauve + a bit of Permanent Blue on others.
9. Highlight these flowers using a #4 flat brush and a mixture of Light Magenta + Brilliant Yellow Light. Tap in dots of Cadmium Yellow Light for the centers using a #1 round brush.
10. Basecoat the peony bud and the lower peony with Burnt Alizarin with a bit of odorless thinner using a #12 flat brush. Overstroke with Light Magenta, then Brilliant Yellow Light, then Brilliant Yellow Light + a bit of Cadmium Orange, and finally with Brillant Yellow Light + a touch of Cerulean Blue. The stroke on the top of the peony is similar to the mum except that the top of the petals are pointed instead of round. The bottom half of the peony is painted with strokes similar to the bottom half of the poppy.
11. Basecoat the large center peony with Light Magenta with a bit of odorless thinner added. Overstroke with Burnt Alizarin + a bit of Floral Mauve, then Brillant Yellow Light, then Brillant Yellow Light + a bit of Cadmium Orange, and finally with Brillant Yellow Light + a bit of Cerulean Blue.
12. Let dry and varnish according to General Instructions.

Mums and Lilacs

Mums and Lilacs

Pattern on Pattern Sheet

Materials

11" x 14" canvas
Palette:
  Permalba—
    Misty Grey
    Burnt Alizarin
    Floral Mauve
  Liquitex—
    Light Magenta
  Shiva—
    Brilliant Yellow Light
  Winsor Newton—
    Indian Yellow
  Grumbacher—
    Permanent Blue
    Raw Sienna
    Cadmium Orange
    Cadmium Yellow Light
    Sap Green
Brushes:
  Blender
  #8 bristle filbert
  #10 flat
  #4 flat
  #1 round

Instructions

1. Transfer pattern to canvas.
2. Using a #8 filbert bristle brush, apply Misty Grey to background, covering the leaf and lilac areas.
3. Add a mixture of Sap Green + a bit of Burnt Alizarin around the design area. Use an "X" stroke and blend the color out over the gray until the color fades out. Soften with a blender brush.
4. Basecoat the larger leaves according to the General Instructions using a #10 flat brush and a mixture of Sap Green + a bit of Burnt Alizarin + a bit of Permanent Blue.
5. Highlight the leaves with Brilliant Yellow Light + Cadmium Yellow Light, then Brilliant Yellow Light + a bit of Cerulean Blue, and finally with Brilliant Yellow Light + a bit of Cadmium Orange. Leave the areas indicated on the pattern by cross hatches darker.
6. Paint the small leaves with a #10 flat brush and the leaf basecoat mixture.
7. Fill in the lilac areas with a mixture of Burnt Alizarin + Floral Mauve + a bit of Permanent Blue using a #10 flat brush.
8. Make four-stroke flowers over the lilac area using a #4 flat brush and Light Magenta + Brilliant Yellow Light, and then Cerulean Blue + Brilliant Yellow Light. Randomly add small dots of Cadmium Yellow Light to the small flower centers using a #1 round brush.
9. Basecoat the mums using a #10 flat brush and Indian Yellow that has a bit of odorless thinner added to it.
10. Paint random "V" strokes of Raw Sienna on the mums.
11. Now overstroke the mums with Brilliant Yellow Light, then Brilliant Yellow Light + a bit of Burnt Alizarin, and finally with Brilliant Yellow Light + a bit of Cadmium Orange. Use a #10 flat brush turned to the side, contouring your strokes to follow the ball shape of the top of the mum. See photograph.
12. Let dry and varnish according to General Instructions.

Victorian Violets

Pattern on Pattern Sheet

Materials
5" x 7" canvas
Palette:
 Winsor Newton—
  Winsor Violet
  Olive Green
 Permalba—
  Floral Mauve
 Grumbacher—
  Soft Formula Titanium White
  Cadmium Yellow Light
  Chromium Oxide Green
Brushes:
 Blender
 #8 bristle filbert
 #4 flat

Instructions
1. Transfer pattern to canvas.
2. Paint the background area with varying mixtures of White, Winsor Violet, and Floral Mauve. All of the mixing is done with a brush on the canvas to keep the color loose. Start on the right side using a #8 bristle filbert and add just a pinch of Floral Mauve and Winsor Violet to the White paint. Apply to the canvas using an "X" stroke. As you move to the left, use less White in the mixture and more Floral Mauve and Winsor Violet. Soften all colors with the blender brush.
3. Fill in the leaves following the General Instructions using Chromium Oxide Green and a #4 flat brush.
4. Darken the leaves at the base where indicated on the pattern by cross hatches with a brush mixture of Olive Green + Winsor Violet. Highlight the leaves with a brush mixture of White + Cadmium Yellow Light + a bit of Chromium Oxide Green.
5. Paint the stems and calyx the same colors as the leaves.
6. Basecoat the violets and buds with Floral Mauve with a bit of odorless thinner added to it. Use a #4 flat brush and stroke in each petal toward the center of the flower, starting at the outside edge.
7. Highlight the violets and buds with a brush mixture of White + a touch of Floral Mauve. Use the same stroke as when you filled in the petals, only end each stroke about halfway toward the center.
8. Paint the flower centers with dots of Cadmium Yellow Light tapped on with the corner of a #4 flat brush.
9. Let dry and varnish according to General Instructions.

Daisies of Innocence